PERSPECTIVES

2000

WORK BOOK

LINDA LEE

2

Cover: The Graphics Studio/Gerry Rosentswieg

Heinle & Heinle Publishers is a division of Wadsworth, Inc.

Manufactured in the United States of America.

ISBN 0-8384-2008-7

10 9 8 7 6 5 4 3

Contents

Name _____ Date _____

1 **Apologizing** *(text, exercise 2).* Complete the conversations below. Use an appropriate tense of the verb in parentheses.

1. A: I'm sorry, but I (not/send) ___*haven't sent*___ your check yet.

   B: No problem. I (have) _____ enough money for this week.

   A: That's good. I (put) _____ the check in the mail on Friday, so you should have it by Monday.

2. A: Something has come up, so I (not/be) _____ able to pick you up tomorrow. I hope this (not/cause) _____ a problem for you.

   B: Don't worry about it. I (not/ask) _____ Tanya for a ride for several weeks. She'll probably be able to pick me up.

3. A: I'm sorry that I (not/call) _____ you for such a long time.

   B: Don't worry about it. I (not/have) _____ time to call you either.

4. A: I (mean) _____ to come over yesterday, but I (not/get) _____ home from work until late.

   B: That's all right. I (go) _____ to bed early anyway.

5. A: I hope you (not/be) _____ here long. I (try) _____ to get here earlier, but I got held up[1] in traffic.

   B: Well, I (be) _____ here for three hours.

   A: Oh, come on. You are trying to make me feel guilty. I know you (not/be) _____ here long.

   B: How (you/know) _____ that?

[1]get held up – be delayed

A: I (call) _____ your house ten minutes ago, and according to your wife, you (just/leave) _____ the house.

6. A: (you/not/clean up) _____ your room yet? What's the matter?
   B: I'm sorry, Mom. I (just/start) _____ to do it when Bruno came over.
   A: I think I (hear) _____ that story before.

2 **Give an example** *(text, exercise 3).* Read each of the sentences below. Then give an example to support the information in the sentence.

1. Homonyms are words that sound alike but have different meanings.
   For example, the words "knows" and "nose" are homonyms.
2. Money can't buy everything.
   _____
3. There are several things you can do to stay healthy.
   _____
4. Not all countries have a president.
   _____
5. Dictionaries contain many kinds of information in addition to word meanings.
   _____
6. There are many beautiful places to visit in my country.
   _____
7. There are a number of excellent writers from my country.
   _____
8. Some rivers go through more than one country.
   _____

3 **Transition words** *(text, exercise 3).* Complete each of the sentences with one of these transition words: *however, for example, moreover.*

1. My friend Gary can play the piano; _____*moreover*_____, he is a wonderful guitar player.
2. My friend Dominque can't play any musical instruments; _____, he can sing beautifully.
3. Louis has been taking guitar lessons for several years; _____, he still can't play very well.

4. Oswaldo is an excellent dancer; _____, he can play the piano.

5. My cousin is a very good athlete; _____, he is the star of the school basketball team.

6. My brother is very good at repairing cars; _____, he knows a lot about fixing things around the house.

7. There are a number of courses I would like to take in school this year; _____, I really want to take a computer course.

8. My grandfather wrote short stories for magazines; _____, he never wrote a book.

9. I try to get some exercise every day; _____, I often go swimming in the morning before breakfast.

10. If you have a question about literature, you should ask Sarah; _____, she can tell you a lot about American history.

4 | **What have you been doing lately?** *(text, exercise 4).* Complete these sentences with either the present perfect continuous or the past perfect continuous tense.

1. I (take) ___*had been taking*___ piano lessons all year, but then my teacher moved away.

2. For the past year, Corine (go) _____ to school to take courses in botany.

3. Alfredo (take care of) _____ his nephews for the past week while his brother is on vacation.

4. Mary Ann (work) _____ in San Diego, but then the company went out of business.

5. Kip (build) _____ a boat for the past year.

6. Stephen (travel) _____ around the country before classes started last week.

7. My brother (go) _____ to night school all year so that he can work during the day.

8. Since my brother bought a house, he (spend) _____ a lot of time fixing it up.

9. Before classes began last month, I (go) _____ fishing and swimming every day.

10. What have you been doing lately?

_____

_____

5   **Indefinite pronouns** *(text, exercise 5).* Underline the correct indefinite pronoun to complete each sentence.

1. Do you know (<u>anyone</u>, somebody) who can tutor me in English?
2. I don't want to go (anywhere, nowhere) today.
3. Did you say (nothing, something)?
4. If (someone, no one) were home, they would answer the phone.
5. I didn't see (nothing, anything) unusual when I drove by her house.
6. (Someone, Anyone) is calling you.
7. (Nowhere, Anywhere) else in the world could I be so happy.
8. What are we going to do if (anybody, nobody) comes to the party?

6   **Subject and verb agreement** *(text, exercise 5).* Underline the correct verb to complete each sentence.

1. Everyone who (<u>takes</u>, take) this course has to buy a book.
2. No one except my sisters (is, are) able to ride that horse.
3. Some of my best friends (is, are) coming to visit next week.
4. Anything (is, are) better than staying home alone.
5. A few of the students (wants, want) to take the test again.
6. I don't know anyone who (writes, write) better than you.
7. I don't think anyone (has, have) ever asked me that question.
8. We will have to go out because there (isn't, aren't) anything in the house to eat.

7   **Identifying or non-identifying?** *(text, exercise 6).* Decide if the clauses in the sentences below are identifying or non-identifying clauses. Write "I" next to the identifying clauses. Write "NI" next to the non-identifying clauses and add commas.

_____ 1. If you see a movie that you like, let me know.

_____ 2. My sister is going to move to Pasadena which is not far from Los Angeles.

_____ 3. I would like you to meet Spencer Davidson who is the current manager of of Turnstyle Engineering.

_____ 4. They live in a house that doesn't have electricity.

_____ 5. My favorite play is Shakespeare's *The Tempest* which was his last play.

_____ 6. Mr. Vitale who retired last month because of health problems is now living in Florida.

_____ 7. The biologist who wrote the report has agreed to come to the meeting.

_____ 8. I can't believe it! I lost the money that you gave me.

Name _____   Date _____

8 **Acronyms** *(text, exercise 6).* An acronym is a word that is made from the first letters of the name of an organization. For example, the acronym NATO stands for the **N**orth **A**tlantic **T**reaty **O**rganization. Read about some additional acronyms in the sentences below. Fill in the blanks with *who, which,* or *that.*

1. CARE (Cooperative for American Relief Everywhere) is the name of an organization ____*that*____ sends packages of food and clothing to people in different parts of the world.

2. VISTA (Volunteers in Service to America) is an organization of people _____ offer their time to help with problems in the United States. For example, a VISTA volunteer may work with people _____ want to learn to read.

3. WHO (World Health Organization), _____ is located in Geneva, Switzerland, is a United Nations organization _____ works to improve health standards around the world.

4. AMVETS (American Veterans of World War II, Korea, and Vietnam) is an organization of people _____ are veterans of World War II, Korea, and Vietnam.

5. If you are a writer, you might want to join ASCAP, _____ is an organization of composers, writers, and publishers in the United States.

6. People _____ think they are working in unsafe conditions should contact OSHA, _____ is the Occupational Safety and Health Administration. This organization, _____ sets safety standards for companies, is part of the United States government.

7. People _____ belong to MADD (Mothers Against Drunk Driving) are working to educate others about the dangers of drinking and driving.

8. NOW, or the National Organization of Women, works to change the laws _____ discriminate against women.

9. A soldier _____ leaves his military base without permission is AWOL, or absent without leave.

10. Many people have seen things in the sky _____ they cannot identify. We call them UFO's, or unidentified flying objects.

9 **Can you identify these?** *(text, exercise 6).* Match the words on the left with their definitions on the right. Write the letter of the definition on the line next to the word. Check your answers by looking up the words in a dictionary.

  e   **1.** audience

____ **2.** auditorium

____ **3.** audiologist

____ **4.** audiovisuals

____ **5.** audition

____ **6.** an audible sound

____ **7.** an inaudible sound

____ **8.** audiometer

a. a test of someone who sings or performs

b. an instrument that measures a person's hearing

c. educational materials that present information in films, tapes, etc.

d. a person who studies hearing

e. a group of people who are listening to or watching a performance

f. something that you cannot hear

g. the room in which people sit while they are listening to or watching a performance

h. something that you can hear

10 **Editing.** There is a mistake in some of the sentences below. Underline the mistake and then write the sentence correctly. Write **Correct** on the line under the sentences with no mistakes.

1. The men, which are standing over there, want to talk with you.

   The men who are standing over there want to talk with you.

2. What are you going to do after you finished this program?

_____

3. Everyone have enough work to do.

_____

4. I waited here for a long time, but she still hasn't called.

_____

5. If she was sick, she would call and tell me.

_____

6. I will wear a coat if I were you.

_____

7. Before you take a test, is a good idea to read it over.

_____

8. One of the students in the class were laughing during the test.

_____

9. While she was waiting for the bus to come, she saw a car accident.

_____

10. She wrote a letter and sent it to they.

_____

11. When I had twelve years old, I went to school in the United States.

_____

12. She bought another boat less expensive.

_____

13. He told to his friends that he wasn't feeling well.

_____

14. She explained at her friends that she had to leave.

_____

15. When the class end, everyone went home.

_____

11 **Vocabulary.** Choose the best answer to complete the sentence or to answer the question. Circle the letter of your answer.

  1. Wendy thinks that making jewelry is **painstaking** work. She says,
    a. "You must do it very slowly and very carefully."
    b. "It hurts a lot to do this work."
    c. "It takes away any pain you feel."

  2. Dario **made an effort** to do his homework. In other words, he
    a. gave up doing his homework.
    b. couldn't do his homework.
    c. tried to do his homework.

  3. Leila wants to **broaden** her knowledge of languages. What is she likely to do?
    a. study several languages
    b. stop studying languages
    c. practice her native language

4. Some people collect **miniature** cars. What do you think they do with these cars?
   a. They drive them.
   b. They put them on a shelf.
   c. They park them on the street.

5. Why would you want to **get hold of** a telephone book?
   a. to keep it from getting lost
   b. for exercise
   c. to find someone's telephone number

6. He read the words **over and over**. In other words, he
   a. read the word twice
   b. repeated the words once
   c. read the words many times

7. Which of these do you need in order to take care of your **correspondence**?
   a. a pen
   b. a knife
   c. a sweater

8. He ate the **entire** pizza before I got there. I asked,
   a. "Why didn't you eat the pizza?"
   b. "Why didn't you leave me some?"
   c. "Is the whole pizza for me?"

9. George thinks that memorizing information is not an **effective** way to study. He says,
   a. "It's the best way to study."
   b. "It won't help you very much."
   c. "It's a useful way to learn."

10. Isabelle wants to stay here **permanently**. She says,
   a. "I'm going to stay here for one more year."
   b. "I am never going to leave this place."
   c. "I can't wait to move."

11. Setsuko plans to **revise** her composition. She says,
   a. "I'm going to read it again and then hand it in."
   b. "I'm going to make some changes to this composition."
   c. "I've finished this composition."

Name _____   Date _____

12 **Writing.** Tell about yourself by answering these questions. Use complete sentences.

1. What kinds of writing do you do outside of school? _____
   _____
   _____

2. When was the last time you wrote a letter? What was your purpose for writing?_____
   _____
   _____

3. What kinds of writing did you have to do in high school? _____
   _____
   _____

4. What was the longest paper you wrote in school? (Give the purpose and length of the paper.)
   _____
   _____

5. What do you do when you can't think of anything to write about? _____
   _____
   _____

6. What kind of writing assignment do you like most? _____
   _____
   _____

7. What kinds of writing practice do you think you need? _____
   _____
   _____

   Freewriting, or writing nonstop for several minutes, is one way to get started writing. Freewriting helps you to get warmed up and to get your ideas flowing. In freewriting, you don't have to worry about making mistakes. The important thing is just to write whatever comes into your head.

   On a separate piece of paper, practice freewriting. For five minutes, just write whatever comes into you mind about school. Don't think about what you are writing. Don't evaluate or correct what you are writing. Just write.

13 **Pairwork.** Work with a partner to make sentences with the words below. Make as many sentences as you can. You may use only the words below, but you can use a word more than once in each sentence.

the	who	was	my
a	person	that	brother
book	is	on	John
desk	took	here	's

_____

_____

_____

_____

_____

_____

_____

_____

_____

_____

Name _____   Date _____

1   **Unusual environments** *(text, exercise 2).* The sentences below describe the planets in our solar system. Complete the sentences with the present tense and either the active or passive voice of the verbs in parentheses.

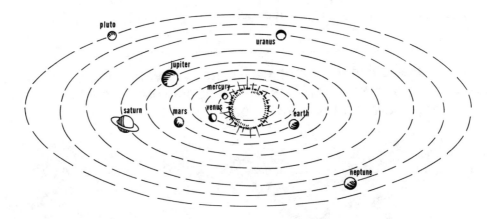

1. Mercury, which (be) _____ *is* _____ the closest planet to the sun, (make)
   _____ *is made* _____ mostly of rock. Like the earth's moon, Mercury (cover)
   _____ with craters, or bowl-shaped holes.

2. The planet Venus (be) _____ about the same size as Earth. It (surround) _____ by thick clouds, which trap the heat. As a result,
   Venus (be) _____ the hottest of the sun's planets.

3. Like Mercury and Venus, the planet Earth (make) _____ of rock.
   However, much of its surface (cover) _____ by water.

4. Mars (be) _____ about half the size of Earth. Its surface (cover)
   _____ by craters, mountains, and the largest volcano in the solar
   system.

5. The planet Jupiter (form) _____ of frozen gases. It also (have)
   _____ a large red spot on its surface, which (be)
   _____ a storm that has been taking place for years.

6. The planet Saturn, which (make) _____ of frozen gases, (surround)
   _____ by seven rings that (make) _____ of dust
   and ice.

7. Uranus is another planet that (make) _____ of frozen gases and that (surround) _____ by rings.

8. Neptune (be) _____ about the same size as Uranus. While it (make) _____ of frozen gases, it (not/have) _____ rings.

9. The smallest planet (be) _____ Pluto, which (probably/make) _____ of ice and rock.

2 **Would you like to live in Biosphere II?** *(text, exercise 2).* The sentences below suggest what life is like inside Biosphere II. Complete the sentences with the present tense and either the active or passive voice.

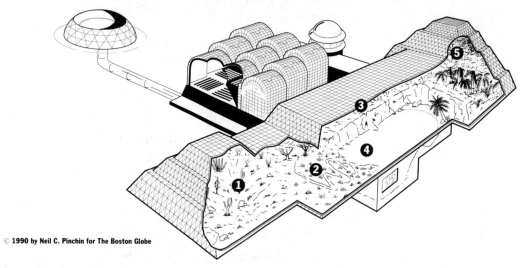

© 1990 by Neil C. Pinchin for The Boston Globe

1. When the doors of Biosphere II are closed, no one (allow) ___*is allowed*___ to leave or enter the structure.

2. The Biospherians—the people who live in Biosphere II—(communicate) _____ with the outside world via computer, telephone, and video.

3. Letters from friends and relatives (send) _____ to the Biospherians via computer.

4. The Biospherians (have) _____ movies to watch and newspapers to read.

5. Each person's health (watch) _____ carefully by scientists on the outside.

6. Each resident (have) _____ a separate apartment.

7. There (be) _____ an exercise room, a lounge, and a library.

8. All of the food for the Biospherians (raise) _____ on a half-acre plot of land.

Name _____   Date _____

9. The Biospherians (be) _____ able to go scuba diving in Biosphere
   II's ocean. This ocean (have) _____ about 1000 different species of
   fish.

10. If they want to go for long walks, the Biospherians (have to) _____
    walk in circles.

11. If a machine stops working, it (repair) _____ by one of the
    Biospherians.

12. Because they have a lot of work to do, no one inside Biosphere II (have)
    _____ time to get bored.

3   **Foods of the future** *(text, exercises 3 and 4).* Complete the sentences with an
appropriate tense and voice of the verb in parentheses. Some of the sentences will
require modals.

1. The apple trees of tomorrow (cut) ___*might be cut*___ into a square shape. If the
   trees are square, machines (be) _____ able to pick the fruit more
   easily. It (be) _____ easier to spray the trees too.

2. The hamburger of tomorrow (not/make) _____ of meat. Instead, it
   (make) _____ of soybeans.

3. Most of the cheese that we eat today (make) _____ from milk. In the
   future, vegetable fat (use) _____ to make cheese.

4. Today more than 90 percent of the soybeans used in the United States (not/eat)
   _____ by people. Instead, these soybeans (eat)
   _____ by pigs and chickens. Because soybeans are high in protein,
   they (become) _____ an important part of our diet in the future.

5. Another food that you (find) _____ on your plate in the future is the
   buffalo gourd. Today the buffalo gourd plant (grow) _____ in very
   dry climates. Inside each of the round yellow gourds (be) _____
   hundreds of seeds. These seeds (grind) _____ into cereal.

6. Many scientists are excited about a plant called the winged bean, which (now/grow) _____ in parts of Southeast Asia. The plant (be) _____ very high in protein, and all parts of the plant (eat) _____.

7. Triticale (be) _____ a hybrid grain of wheat and rye. Triticale may be a food of the future for many people because it (plant) _____ in sandy, poor soils.

4 **Conversations** *(text, exercises 2 and 4).* Complete the conversations below. Use an appropriate tense and voice of the verb in parentheses.

1. A: Excuse me. Could you tell me where the supplies (keep) _____*are kept*_____ ? I (need) _____ to get some paper.
   B: Let me show you. Everything (store) _____ in these cabinets. If you can't find what you need here, we (order) _____ it.

2. A: My car (break down[1]) _____. Can you give me a ride home?
   B: Sorry. My car (repair) _____ today.

3. A: Did you know that the old train station (tear down) _____ next month?
   B: It's terrible, isn't it? It's such a beautiful old building. They (build) _____ a modern shopping center in its place.

4. A: Do you know when the mail (usually/deliver) _____?
   B: The mailman usually (get) _____ here around ten. (you/expect) _____ something important?
   A: You'd better believe it. I hope (get) _____ my check. If my bills (not/pay) _____ soon, I'm going to be in big trouble.

[1]break down – stop working; stop functioning

5. A: What film (show) _____ downtown?

   B: I'm not sure. Why (you/not/look) _____ in the newspaper?

6. A: I hear that next week's soccer game (play) _____ here.

   B: Really? Where (you/hear) _____ that?

   A: Paul (tell) _____ me. According to him, the other team's field

   (tear up) _____, so we can't play there.

5 **What is the result?** *(text, exercise 5).* Match the "if" clauses on the left with the result clauses on the right.

_e_ **1.** If you drive too fast,	**a.**	you will miss the test.
____ **2.** If you had a car,	**b.**	you will have more energy.
____ **3.** If you don't come to class today,	**c.**	you would do better in class.
____ **4.** If you eat something,	**d.**	she would be surprised.
____ **5.** If you need a ride,	**e.**	the police might stop you.
____ **6.** If you studied more,	**f.**	he will get sick.
____ **7.** If you called her,	**g.**	you could give me a ride home.
____ **8.** If he eats all of that,	**h.**	you can come with me.

6 **Editing.** There is a mistake in some of the sentences below. Underline the mistake and then write the sentence correctly. Write **Correct** on the line under the sentences with no mistakes.

1. Since I was twelve years old, I <u>was interested</u> in sports.
   Since I was twelve years old, I have been interested in sports.

2. He went out without his parent permission.

   _____

3. He tries to live his life without hurt anyone.

   _____

4. He left the country on March.

   _____

5. When I got home, I found out that he has already done all of the work.

   _____

6. I want to say something about my father, that his name is Francisco.

   _____

7. I've been looking for his address, but I can't find it.

_____

8. I need that somebody give me a ride to school.

_____

9. I have a friend that she studies in Peru.

_____

10. Last Friday my father returns home from his trip.

_____

11. If I could write to him, I will invite him to come here.

_____

12. He being paid by the government to do a study of the area.

_____

13. Biosphere II, that is located in Arizona, will be completely self-sufficient.

_____

14. Everyone who live in Biosphere II will have to work hard.

_____

15. As soon as he gets back, I will feel much better.

_____

7 **Writing.** When you are writing something, it's helpful to think about why you are writing and about who will read it. Read the note below and then answer the questions.

> *4 P.M.*
>
> *Joe,*
>
> *I won't be back until six. If Janine calls, tell her that I'll pick her up at eight tomorrow morning.*
>
> *See you in a little while.*
>
> *Love you,*
> *Carol*

1. What is Carol's reason for writing the note? _____

_____

2. What do you think Joe's relationship with Carol is? How do you know this? _____

_____

Now follow the instructions below each box. As you write each note, think about your reason for writing it and about who will read it.

Write a note in the box to invite a good friend to do something.

Write a short letter in the box to invite a person who is well known in politics or the arts to come to speak to your class. Show your notes to a classmate and talk about how they are the same or different.

8 **Vocabulary.** Choose the best answer to complete the sentence or answer the question. Circle the letter of your answer.

1. Which of these statements might be made by an **environmentalist**?
   a. "Recycling is unnecessary."
   b. "We must stop polluting the environment."
   c. "We don't have to do anything about pollution."

2. Anne lives in the **suburbs**. She says,
   a. "I have to drive for hours to get to the city."
   b. "I live in the center of the city."
   c. "I live just outside of the city."

3. Jack is worried about the environment, but he thinks that **things are looking up**. He says,
   a. "Air pollution is getting worse."
   b. "More people are trying to do something about pollution."
   c. "Many people are polluting the environment."

4. Michael is **self-sufficient**. He says,
   a. "My parents help me to pay the rent."
   b. "I take care of all my bills."
   c. "I can't pay my bills because I don't have a job."

5. Which of these is not an example of a **structure**?
   a. a house
   b. a carpet
   c. a birdhouse

6. According to Deborah, the test was **tough**. She said,
   a. "It was not an easy test."
   b. "I finished it quickly."
   c. "The test was easy."

7. Nadine has **cut down on** the amount of sugar she eats. She says,
   a. "I have quit eating sugar."
   b. "I am eating less sugar these days."
   c. "I don't like sweet things any more."

8. Which of these is not an **annual** event?
   a. Christmas
   b. someone's birthday
   c. a full moon

9. Which of these is an example of **wastefulness**?
   a. using a cup once and throwing it away
   b. recycling newspapers
   c. reusing plastic knives and forks

10. Fernando wants to **carpool** to work. He says to his friend,
   a. "You drive today, and I'll drive tomorrow."
   b. "We should take the bus to work."
   c. "Let's each take our car to work."

9 **Word forms.** Choose the correct form of the word to complete each of the sentences below. Write the word on the blank line. Make any necessary changes in the form and tense of the verb.

1. suburbs   suburban
   A: I have finally decided to move out to the _____*suburbs*_____.
   B: Do you think you will like living in a _____ area?

2. production   produce
   A: All of their food _____ on their farm.
   B: Who is in charge of the _____ of food?

3. encouragement   encourage
   A: What did you do _____ your brother to go back to school?
   B: He didn't need my _____. He decided on his own to go back.

4. waste   wasteful
   A: Let's ride our bikes to the store instead of taking the car. I don't want _____ gasoline.
   B: You're right. It's _____ to use the car just to go to the store.

5. enclosure   enclose
   A: Why did you _____ your back yard?
   B: I wanted to make an _____ for the dog to run around in.

6. employees   employ
   A: How many people _____ in your office?
   B: I think there are about 60 _____.

10 **Pairwork.** Think of three things that you use every day. On the lines below, write three sentences that give information about each object. However, do not identify the object. You may, for example, say what it is made of, how often it is used, when it is used, and where it is used. Exchange papers with a classmate and guess what your partner's objects are.

1. You write here:_____
   _____
   _____

What is it? Your partner answers here:_____

2. You write here:_____
   _____
   _____

What is it? Your partner answers here:_____

3. You write here:_____
   _____
   _____

What is it? Your partner answers here:_____

Name _____   Date _____

The Olympic Games

1 **The Special Olympics and the Torch Run** *(text, exercise 2).* Complete the sentences below with the simple present or past tense of the verbs in parentheses; use either the active or passive voice.

1. The Special Olympics is a year-round sports-training program for children and adults with mental retardation. It (develop) *___was developed___* to give these individuals the opportunity to train for and compete in sports activities.

2. The Special Olympic Games (hold) _____ annually in every state of the United States and in more than 80 other countries.

3. The first games (hold) _____ in 1968.

4. The athletes who participate in the Special Olympics (coach) _____ throughout the year by volunteers.

5. To raise money for the Special Olympics, a Torch Run (organize) _____ in each state.

6. Police officers in each state (agree) _____ to run a certain number of miles. One officer (carry) _____ a torch as he or she runs. After running a certain distance, the officer (pass) _____ the torch to another officer. In this way, the torch (pass) _____ from officer to officer.

7. Money (collect) _____ from the people in each town to support the police officers who participate in the Torch Run.

8. More than $7 million (raise) _____ by the Torch Run between 1985 and 1990.

9. The first Torch Run (make up of) _____ five police officers.

10. Today more than 50,000 police officers (participate) _____ in the Torch Run.

2 **Famous firsts** *(text, exercise 2).* Complete these sentences with the simple past tense of the verbs in parentheses, using either the passive or active voice.

1. The first newsreel (show) ___*was shown*___ in a movie theater in 1910. However, moving pictures of historic events (take) _____ earlier. For example, a film (make) _____ of President McKinley's inaugural parade in 1896.

2. The first talking picture (present) _____ to the public in 1926. Sound (not/record) _____ on the film. Instead, the film (accompany) _____ by music from phonograph records.

3. The first talking picture that (film) _____ outdoors was *In Old Arizona*. Most of this movie (make) _____ in Utah and in California.

4. The first fully enclosed sports arena (build) _____ in 1963 in Houston, Texas. It (hold) _____ 48,000 people.

5. Volleyball (develop) _____ in 1895 by William Morgan of the YMCA. At first the game (call) _____ "Mintonette." There were no nets in the early games. Instead, a piece of rope (place) _____ across the court.

6. Modern basketball (invent) _____ by James Naismith in 1892. When the game (play) _____ in those days, one of the players (have to) _____ use a ladder to remove the ball from the basket.

7. The first motorcycle (design) _____ by the E.R. Thomas Motor Co. of New York in 1900. They simply (attach) _____ a single-cylinder gas engine to a bicycle.

8. A pair of ice skates that (find) _____ in France may be 20,000 years old. These skates (make) _____ of animal bones. Steel blades for ice skates (not/invent) _____ until 1848.

9. The first person on the moon (be) _____ Neil Armstrong. Armstrong also (bring) _____ the first lunar rocks to Earth.

10. The first successful man-powered aircraft (design) _____ by Paul MacCready, an aeronautical engineer. Bryan Allen (fly) _____ the aircraft over a 3-mile course in 1977.

3 **An experiment** *(text, exercise 2).* The passive is used frequently in scientific and technical writing. This is because the focus is on what happened rather than on who did it. Change this report of an experiment into the passive.

1. The experimenter suspended a magnet so that it hung about one foot above a table.

   A magnet was suspended so that it hung about one foot above a table.

2. The experimenter tied a metal paper clip to a thin piece of string.

   _____

   _____

3. The experimenter held the loose end of the string down on the table with a heavy book.

   _____

   _____

4. The experimenter allowed the string to extend far enough so that the paper clip was within half an inch of the hanging magnet.

   _____

   _____

5. The experimenter held the magnet so that it did not swing.

   _____

   _____

6. The experimenter released the paper clip and the magnet.

   _____

   _____

   Here are the results of the experiment:

   The paper clip floated in mid-air without any visible means of support. The magnet attracted the paper clip, but the clip and the magnet could not touch because the string held the paper clip back.

4 **Things to do** *(text, exercise 3).* Before I left on my trip, I made a list of things to do. Then, I checked off each item as I did it. Complete the sentences to explain what has or has not been done so far.

> ### *Things to do*
>
> √ **feed the dog**
> √ **close the windows**
>   **lock the front door**
>   **take out the trash**
> √ **pack the suitcases**
>   **turn off all the lights**
>   **wash the dishes**
> √ **water the plants**
> √ **turn the heat down**
>   **turn on the telephone**
>   **answering machine**
> √ **call George about**
>   **picking up the mail**
>   **pay the bills**
>   **fill up the car (with gas)**

---

1. The dog _____ *has been fed* _____.
2. The windows _____.
3. The front door _____.
4. The trash _____.
5. The suitcases _____.
6. The lights _____.
7. The dishes _____.
8. The plants _____.
9. The heat _____.
10. The telephone answering machine _____.
11. George _____.
12. The bills _____.
13. The car _____.

5 **Conversations** *(text, exercise 3).* Complete the conversations below. Use an appropriate tense and voice of the verb in parentheses. More than one answer may be correct.

1. A: You don't have to go to school today.

   B: Why not?

   A: Classes (just/cancel) *have just been canceled* .

2. A: You're late. I hope you (already/eat) _____.

   B: No, I haven't. And I'm starving.

   A: Uh oh. All of the food (eat) _____.

3. A: What do we have to do to get ready for the party?

   B: Nothing. Everything (do) _____.

   A: Everything?

   B: Yes, everything. The house (already/clean) _____ and the food
      (cook) _____.

4. A: I (feed) _____ the animals.

   B: You did? So did I.

   A: Well, I guess they (feed) _____ twice.

5. A: Where did you find this book?

   B: Over there. It (bury) _____ under that pile of papers.

6. A: How long has the polio vaccine been around?

   B: It (develop) _____ in 1954.

   A: This vaccine (take) _____ orally, wasn't it?

   B: No, the oral vaccine (not/use) _____ until 1961.

6 **What's the solution?** *(text, exercise 4).* Complete the sentences below using *will, can, might, should, must,* or *have (has) to.* Use either the active or the passive voice. More than one correct answer is possible.

1. A: What are you going to do with all of these old newspapers?
   B: I don't know. They really (throw) *should be thrown* away.

2. A: I think the tree in the front yard is dying.
   B: I think you're right. It really (cut down) _____.

3. A: Why can't you come with us tomorrow?
   B: I (finish) _____ painting the kitchen.

4. A: You'd better slow down. This road is terrible.
   B: It sure is. This road (repair) _____.

5. A: I'm really sorry that I missed that movie.
   B: Don't get upset. It (show) _____ again next week, so you can see it then.

6. A: It's late. Why are you still studying?
   B: I'm not sure, but I think we (have) _____ a quiz tomorrow. I want to be prepared.

7. A: If you want this letter to arrive on time, it (mail) _____ today.
   B: Thanks for reminding me.

8. A: I followed your directions carefully, but I still got lost.
   B: I don't think my directions were very clear. They really (rewrite)
   _____.

9. A: Mrs. Liu called while you were out.
   B: Thanks for telling me. I (call) _____ her back before she leaves for work.

10. A: Something in the refrigerator smells bad!
    B: I know. The refrigerator really (clean) _____ out.

Name _____ Date _____

7 **Editing.** There is a mistake in some of the sentences below. Underline the mistake and then write the sentence correctly. Write **Correct** on the line under the sentences with no mistakes.

1. Everyone in the class <u>were</u> able to come on the picnic.
   Everyone in the class was able to come on the picnic.

2. If he were here now, I would ask him come with us.
   _____

3. If it doesn't stop raining soon, we wouldn't be able to go outside.
   _____

4. My aunt is the person that she lived in Venezuela in the 1960s.
   _____

5. They haven't been to the city for more than a month.
   _____

6. He went home because classes had been cancelled.
   _____

7. Someone have been trying to call you.
   _____

8. Francisco and me have been working on this car for hours.
   _____

9. San Francisco, that is in California, is a popular tourist spot.
   _____

10. The pictures that he showed us was from his trip to Hawaii.
    _____

11. He left the country on June, but he plans to come back soon.
    _____

12. Before he got sick, he enjoyed to swim each morning.
    _____

13. If he wasn't so lazy, he would be able to get a good job.
    _____

14. As soon as the picture was took, everyone started talking.
    _____

15. When he moved away, he gave all of his things to George and I.
    _____

Vocabulary. Choose the best answer to complete the statements or to answer the questions. Circle the letter of your answer.

1. Janine is **boycotting** the shoe store downtown. She says,
   a. "I'm going to buy all of my shoes from that store."
   b. "I refuse to buy anything from that store."
   c. "I encourage everyone to buy their shoes from that store."

2. Mauricio was **inspired** by his brother to climb the mountain. He said,
   a. "My brother did it, so I thought maybe I could too."
   b. "My brother told me I couldn't do it."
   c. "My brother would never climb a mountain."

3. Ernesto is **in charge of** the soccer team. In other words,
   a. he is the fastest runner on the team.
   b. he is the best player on the team.
   c. he is responsible for the team.

4. Classes were **suspended** for an hour. In other words,
   a. there were no classes for an hour.
   b. classes were held for an hour only.
   c. after an hour of classes, everyone went home.

5. Alex is not a very **competitive** person. He says,
   a. "I only like to compete when I am sure I can win."
   b. "I don't care if I win or lose."
   c. "I don't like to participate in anything."

6. Everyone who works in the factory is **required** to wear a hard hat. After Philip gets a job in the factory, he says,
   a. "I might have to wear a hard hat."
   b. "I have to wear a hard hat."
   c. "I must not wear a hard hat."

7. Short skirts are **popular** today. In other words,
   a. many women are wearing short skirts today.
   b. no one likes to wear short skirts anymore.
   c. someone is wearing a short skirt today.

8. Which of these is an example of a **continent**?
   a. California
   b. France
   c. Asia

Name _____ Date _____

9. George was the **winner** of the race. He
   a. came in first.
   b. didn't finish the race.
   c. organized the race.

10. Laura **admitted** to her mistake. She said,
    a. "I don't think I made a mistake."
    b. "It was George's mistake."
    c. "I made a mistake."

11. At Jorge's school, they are going to **eliminate** French from the course offerings. In other words,
    a. they are going to add French to the course offerings.
    b. they will no longer offer French courses.
    c. they will give more French courses.

12. Sandro **participated** in the soccer match. In other words, he
    a. watched the game.
    b. criticized the game.
    c. played in the game.

9 **Word forms.** Choose the word that best completes each sentence. Make any necessary changes in the verbs.

1. **introduction   introduce**
   A: Do you want me ___*to introduce*___ you to my brother?
   B: We don't need an _____. We met last weekend.

2. **cancellation   cancel**
   A: I hear the games _____ because of the rain.
   B: I know. Their _____ is going to upset a lot of people.

3. **presentation   present**
   A: The _____ of awards took more than an hour.
   B: Really! How many awards _____ ?

4. **participation   participate**
   A: If this program is going to be a success, we need the _____ of everyone in the class.
   B: Do we have to pay _____ ?

5. invitation   invite

A: Did you get my _____ to the party?

B: Yes, thanks for _____ me.

6. demonstration   demonstrate

A: Did you take part in the peace _____ yesterday?

B: You bet. It's the first time I _____ since the 1960s.

7. competition   compete

A: I hear that you _____ in the marathon next week.

B: Yes, but I'm a little nervous. The _____ is supposed to be tough.

10 Writing. Read the paragraph below and follow the instructions.

Every year in October, Americans celebrate Halloween. One popular custom for this holiday is making jack o' lanterns. These Halloween lanterns are easy to make if you have a knife, a pumpkin, and a candle, and if you follow a few simple steps. To make the jack o' lantern, you must <u>first</u> cut the top off the pumpkin. You must cut the top off carefully, however, so that you can replace it later. Next, scoop the seeds out of the pumpkin and throw them away. You are now ready to cut a face into the pumpkin. This face can have eyes, a nose, and a mouth, or it can be more abstract. Last, place a candle inside the pumpkin, light it, and place the top back on the pumpkin. Your jack o' lantern is now ready to be placed on the front steps of your house or in a window. If you have made it correctly, it will scare ghosts and goblins away from your house.

This paragraph explains the steps to follow in order to make a jack o'lantern. The writer of this paragraph used several time signals to help the reader follow the order of the steps. The first time signal is underlined for you. Find the other time signals in the paragraph and underline them.

Now think of something that people in your country make for a specific holiday. You may want to freewrite for a few minutes to get some ideas on paper. Then, write a paragraph explaining to one of your classmates how to make this item. Use some of the time signals below to indicate the order of the steps. When you have finished, ask a classmate to read your paragraph and to answer the questions in the box.

Time signals: *first, second, next, last, finally, then*

_____

_____

_____

_____

_____

_____

_____

_____

_____

_____

Are the ideas clearly expressed?	___ yes	___ no
Is there enough information?	___ yes	___ no
Is the sequence clear?	___ yes	___ no

11 **Pairwork.** Work with a partner to come up with an idea for a simple game to play with children. This could be a game that you played as a child or an invention of your own. Work with your partner to prepare a presentation of the game for the rest of the class.

1 **The job interview** *(text, exercise 2).* What should and shouldn't a person do during a job interview? Each of the people below did something that they probably shouldn't have done. Read the sentences and decide what each person should have done instead. Write your ideas on the blank lines.

1. Maria got to the job interview late because she got caught in traffic.
   She should have left for the interview earlier.

2. When the interviewer asked Ernesto about his future plans, he couldn't think of anything to say.

   _____

3. Philip wore old blue jeans to the interview.

   _____

4. Sarah lied on the job application.

   _____

5. During the interview, Willard gave the impression that he wasn't interested in the job.

   _____

6. Melanie was late to the interview because she got lost.

   _____

7. When the interviewer asked Italo about his previous employer, Italo said some unkind things.

   _____

8. Michael was exhausted at the interview because he had stayed up late the night before.

   _____

Name _____ Date _____

2 **What's the explanation?** *(text, exercises 3 and 4).* Read each of the sentences below and decide on a possible explanation for each situation. Use modals where possible.

1. Our next door neighbors suddenly bought an enormous boat and two new cars.
   They might have won the lottery.

2. When I got to school, no one was there.
   _____

3. I got a bill from a store that I have never heard of.
   _____

4. The telephone company billed me for a telephone call to Puerto Rico, but I don't know anyone in Puerto Rico. I am sure I didn't make this call.
   _____

5. Last night I filled the car with gasoline. When I tried to start the car this morning, the gas tank was empty.
   _____

6. I wrote a letter to you last week, but it was returned to me.
   _____

7. My favorite ski resort went out of business last year.
   _____

8. Jenny was supposed to pick me up today, but she never arrived.
   _____

9. When I got home, all of the fruit from the tree was on the ground.
   _____

10. When I got to work, I discovered that I didn't have my house keys with me.
    _____

3 **Conversations** *(text, exercises 2, 3, and 4).* Complete the conversations using an appropriate tense of the verb in parentheses. In some cases, you will need to use a modal. More than one correct answer may be possible.

1. A: What happened to Paul? He (arrive) _____*should have arrived*_____ by now.
   B: I don't know. He (get) _____ out of class late.
   A: But he doesn't have class today. I think he (forget) _____
      about the meeting.
   B: That's possible. He's pretty forgetful. I guess we (call)
      _____ to remind him.

2. A: Uh oh. I don't have my keys. I (leave) _____ them in the car.

B: Are you sure? You (put) _____ them in your coat pocket. Did you check?

A: No such luck. I (take) _____ them out of the ignition immediately, but I was talking to Sarah.

B: Oh, well. Let's get a coat hanger.

3. A: Are you interested in (go) _____ out tonight?

B: I can't. I have to finish that report.

A: What! You (not/finish) _____ that yet?

B: I know. I know. I (do) _____ it yesterday, but I just wasn't in the mood.[1]

4. A: I think I (turn) _____ right back there.

B: You (not/turn) _____ right. It was a one-way street.

A: Well, I (make) _____ a mistake somewhere because we are lost.

B: Maybe you (stop) _____ at the next gas station. Someone there (be) _____ able to tell us where we are.

5. A: Why are you wearing blue jeans? I think you (put on) _____ a suit and tie.

B: A suit and tie? I thought we were going to a casual party.

A: You (misunderstand) _____. It's a formal party.

B: Really? You (tell) _____ me sooner. My suit's at the cleaners.

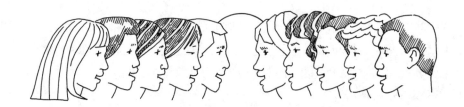

[1]be in the mood – feel like doing something; want to do something

Name _____   Date _____

4 **More hindsight** *(text, exercise 5).* Complete the sentences below.

1. I should have studied for the test. If I ___*had studied for the test*___, I would have done better.

2. He shouldn't have drunk all that coffee. If he _____, he would have been able to get to sleep.

3. I guess I shouldn't have said that. If I _____, she wouldn't have gotten angry.

4. Jorge thinks that he should have learned to use a computer. If he _____, he would have gotten that job.

5. You should have worn a coat. If you _____, you wouldn't have caught a cold.

6. I should have closed the door. If I _____, the dog wouldn't have gotten out.

7. I guess I should have taken the car. If I _____, we wouldn't have been late.

8. I should have put a stamp on the letter.

   _____

   _____

9. I should have called the police right away.

   _____

   _____

10. I guess I shouldn't have put my money in my pocket.

    _____

    _____

5 **What would you have done?** *(text, exercise 5).* Complete these sentences.

1. If I had seen you on the street, ___*I would have stopped to talk.*___

2. If I hadn't taken this English course, _____

   _____

3. If I had learned English as a child, _____

   _____

4. If I had lived one hundred years ago, _____

   _____

5. If I had discovered America, _____

   _____

6. If I had grown up in Australia, _____

_____

7. If I had missed class today, _____

_____

8. If I had done my homework earlier, _____

_____

6 **Editing.** There is a mistake in some of the sentences below. Underline the mistake and then write the sentence correctly. Write **Correct** on the line under the sentences with no mistakes.

1. If I had left earlier, I wouldn't have missed the bus.

_____*Correct*_____

2. If he were sick, I would have gone over to visit him.

_____

3. She is really the most strong person I know.

_____

4. When he comes at home, we will have dinner together.

_____

5. He gave me a book that it has pictures.

_____

6. My father was the person who always takes me to school.

_____

7. I want you understand the whole story.

_____

8. He could have go to the game, but he decided not to.

_____

9. There are several things that we need to talk about.

_____

10. I think we should go to the meeting last week.

_____

11. Everyone who enjoy dancing should buy this new tape.

_____

12. Everyone in the family was upset because my brother had lost his job.

_____

13. I don't know the man that he is in your class.

_____

14. Did he asked you to give a speech?

_____

15. I am not going to say anything until he leaves.

_____

7 **Vocabulary.** Choose the best answer to complete the sentence or to answer the question. Circle the letter of your answer.

1. Simon is a **critic** of bilingual education. He says,
   a. "I don't think bilingual education works."
   b. "I support bilingual education."
   c. "Bilingual education is a part of our school program."

2. According to Paul, his mother is **brilliant**. He says,
   a. "My mother is beautiful."
   b. "My mother is very intelligent."
   c. "My mother is very rich."

3. Luisa was **elated** when she heard the news. She said,
   a. "I'm sorry to hear that."
   b. "I don't really care."
   c. "What wonderful news!"

4. Which of these is the most **time-consuming** task?
   a. washing the dishes
   b. painting a house
   c. washing a car

5. Mauricio told his brother to **hurry** to the bank. He said,
   a. "You should walk."
   b. "Stop and get a cup of coffee on your way to the bank."
   c. "Go as fast as you can."

6. Laura's **ancestors** came from Poland. She says,
   a. "My great-grandparents came from Poland."
   b. "I came from Poland."
   c. "My brothers and sisters came from Poland."

7. His sister **turned down** a job at the United Nations. In other words, she
   a. accepted the job.
   b. refused the job.
   c. gave up the job.

8. Everyone got **soaked** when they went outside. Someone said,

    a. "I wonder when it is going to start raining."

    b. "I almost got wet."

    c. "We should have brought umbrellas."

9. Oswaldo is in **desperate** need of money. He said,

    a. "I need some money urgently."

    b. "I may need some money in the future."

    c. "It would be nice to have more money."

10. Joshua couldn't **resist** the piece of cake that I offered him. He said,

    a. "No, thank you. I'm not hungry."

    b. "I don't like cake."

    c. "I can't say no."

8   **Word forms.** Choose the correct form of the word to complete the dialogue. Make any necessary changes in the verbs.

1. wealth   wealthy

    A: How did he get to be such a ____*wealthy*____ person?

    B: I think that most of his _____ came from his family.

2. discovery   discover

    A: When did they _____ oil there?

    B: I'm not sure but I think the _____ was made in the 1950s.

3. decision   decide

    A: Have you made a _____ yet?

    B: No, I haven't had time _____.

4. explanation   explain

    A: Can you _____ what happened?

    B: No, I really don't have an _____.

5. judgment   judge

    A: How do you _____ which painting is best?

    B: It's not easy to make a _____.

Name _____ Date _____

6. invention   invent

A: What _____ is he famous for?

B: I think he is famous for _____ the ballpoint pen.

7. value   valuable

A: What is the _____ of this bracelet?

B: I don't know for sure, but I am certain it is _____.

Now complete this chart by listing the words in the appropriate category.

Noun	Verb	Adjective
wealth		

9 **Writing.** Reread the paragraph below about William Orton. As you read, think about how the writer connected the sentences in the paragraph. How did he or she connect the second sentence to the third sentence? The fourth sentence to the fifth sentence? Look for the connecting devices listed below and underline them. An example is done for you.

- use of pronouns
- use of synonyms
- use of connecting words and transitions
- repetition of key words

> To some people, William Orton is known as the person who made the worst business decision in American history. In 1877, William Orton was the president of Wetern Union Telegraph Company. That year, Alexander Graham Bell and his partners offered to sell their telephone patents to Western Union. Orton could have bought them for a mere $100,000, but he turned down the offer. After reviewing the patents, Orton commented, "What use could this company make of an electrical toy?" In retrospect, we know that Orton should have bought the patents. He could have made millions of dollars from them because they turned out to be the most valuable patents ever issued.

The sentences below are not tied together very well. Rewrite the second sentence in each pair so that the two sentences are more clearly connected.

1. Like a lot of young people, my brother doesn't think he knows much about anything. My brother knows a lot about the history of his town.

   In fact, he knows a lot about the history of his town.
   _____

2. I live in the suburbs. It's easy to get into the city from the suburbs.

   _____

3. There is pleasure in owning things. There is deeper pleasure in owning fewer things.

   _____

4. My friends don't look at life the way I do. My friends don't talk about the future.

   _____

5. Being sixteen years old isn't easy. At the age of sixteen, a person is confronted with many choices.

   _____

Next, write a paragraph to tell your classmates about one of the topics below. As you write, concentrate on tying the sentences in your paragraph together. Write your final draft of the paragraph on the lines below and ask a classmate to read it and to answer the questions in the box.

- a problem that you think people should be more aware of
- something that is happening in your town now
- a remarkable person whom you think your classmates should know about
- the history of one building in your town

_____
_____
_____
_____
_____
_____
_____
_____
_____
_____
_____

Is the paragraph clear?	___ yes	___ no
Did the writer use any transition words?	___ yes	___ no
Did the writer use pronouns?	___ yes	___ no
Did the writer repeat key words?	___ yes	___ no

10 **Pairwork.** With your partner, come up with a list of things that a person should and should not do at a job interview. Write your ideas on the lines below. Then, role-play a job interview for the rest of the class. Include things from your list of job interview "do's" and "don'ts." Ask your classmates to explain what the people at the interview should have done differently.

1. _____
   _____

2. _____
   _____

3. _____
   _____

4. _____
   _____

5. _____
   _____

6. _____
   _____

7. _____
   _____

8. _____
   _____

9. _____
   _____

10. _____
    _____

1 **Answering questions** *(text, exercise 2).* Have you ever noticed how young children like to ask questions about everything? Think of answers to these children's questions. Use *so (that)* or *in order to* in your answers.

1. A: I don't like these vegetables. Why do I have to eat them?
   B: *You have to eat them to be strong and healthy.*

2. A: Why do I have to brush my teeth?
   B: _____

3. A: I'm not tired, so why do I have to go to bed?
   B: _____

4. A: Why do I have to take vitamins every morning?
   B: _____

5. A: I hate baths. Why do I have to take one?
   B: _____

6. A: Why do I have to go to school?
   B: _____

7. A: If I'm not hungry, why do I have to eat breakfast?
   B: _____

8. A: Please don't make me get a shot.[1] Why do I have to get one?
   B: _____

9. A: Why do you have to go to work every day?
   B: _____

2 **Cause and effect** *(text, exercise 3).* Complete these sentences with an adjective, an adverb, or an adjective + a noun. More than one answer may be correct.

1. It was so _____*windy*_____ yesterday that all of the leaves were blown off the tree.

2. He was driving so _____ that he didn't see the stop sign.

3. His parents gave him so _____ that he never had to get a job.

4. He has such _____ that he can never find shoes that fit.

5. Their new car is so _____ that it won't fit in the garage.

[1]shot – an injection of medicine through a needle

6. He gained so _____ while he was on vacation that he has to go on a diet now.

7. The water in the river was so _____ that all the fish died.

8. The mud was so _____ that the car eventually got stuck in it.

9. It was so _____ last summer that all my plants died.

10. He ate such a _____ that he wasn't hungry for the rest of the day.

11. She opened all of the windows because there was such a _____ in the house.

12. He was so _____ at the end of the day that he went right to bed when he got home.

3 **What is the explanation?** *(text, exercise 4).* Can you explain the actions of the people below? Complete the sentences using *so (that)*, *in order to*, *because, or since.* More than one answer is possible.

1. Yan disconnected the telephone _*because he didn't want to talk to anyone.*_

2. Sydney put all of his books in a box _____
   _____

3. Alice wrote my address on a piece of paper _____
   _____

4. Meg put an extra blanket on the bed _____
   _____

5. Toni hid the candy _____
   _____

6. Philip carefully put the matches in a high place _____
   _____

7. When they moved into the apartment, they put curtains on the windows _____
   _____

8. Pietro pulled the car over to the side of the road _____
   _____

9. I took off my shoes _____
   _____

10. Somchai closed the door quickly _____
    _____

11. Ken didn't answer my letter _____
    _____

4 **Traffic jam** *(text, exercise 5).* Have you ever been caught in a traffic jam? Read the thoughts of the person below, who is stuck in traffic. Match the clauses to make complete sentences.

_e_ **1.** If I have to wait here much longer, I   **a.** would have taken the train.

_____ **2.** If I take a different road tomorrow, I   **b.** wouldn't be so much traffic on this road.

_____ **3.** If I had known the traffic was going to be so bad, I

    c. won't get caught in traffic.

_____ **4.** If fewer people drove to work, there   **d.** would be much happier.

_____ **5.** If I had taken a different road, I   **e.** will be late for dinner.

_____ **6.** If I were at home now, I   **f.** would have missed all of this traffic.

5 **Cause and effect** *(text, exercise 5).* Complete the sentences below. More than one correct answer is possible.

1. At the end of the month, Adeline is complaining because she doesn't have any money. Her brother says, *"If you hadn't gone to the movies so many times, you would have some money."*

2. Julian doesn't like the TV program that he is watching. After listening to him complain for several minutes, his sister says, "If _____

_____."

3. Carlos forgot to stop at the store to get something for dinner. When he gets home, his wife says, "If _____

_____ "

4. George has been waiting for over an hour for his friend Josh to pick him up. Finally George says to himself, "If _____

_____ "

5. Richard's eight-year-old son keeps forgetting to put his bicycle inside at night. Richard decides to talk to him about it. He says to his son, "If _____

_____ "

6. Stephanie was in a car accident last week, but she didn't get hurt because she was wearing her seatbelt. After the accident, Stephanie thought to herself, "If _____

_____ "

7. Danny is trying to convince his brother to help him fix his radio. He says to his brother, "If _____ "

8. Jorge can't decide if he should change jobs, so he asks his friend for advice. His friend says, "If _____

_____ "

6 **Where have they gone?** *(text, exercise 6).* Complete the paragraph below with an appropriate tense of the verb in parentheses and either the active or passive voice.

Human beings (contribute) ___*have contributed*___ to the extinction of valuable resources in several ways. Each year hundreds of billions of tons of pollutants (release) _____ into the environment by humans. These pollutants (destroy) _____ the habitats of an increasing number of species. Many other species (eliminate) _____ by hunters and sportsmen. Since 1600, hunters (cause) _____ the extinction of a variety of species, including many kinds of birds, the Steller's sea cow, eleven species of tortoises, six species of West Indian lizards, and four species of snakes. Another way that valuable species (destroy) _____ is through the introduction of new species into an area. For example, a century ago, American bluebirds (push) _____ out of the area by European starlings. Another example is the brown tree snake, which (carry) _____ from the Philippines to Guam by Navy ships during World War II. That species (already/destroy) _____ most of Guam's native species of birds. For instance, the number of Guam rails (drop) _____ from forty thousand to eighteen in just twenty-five years. In Hawaii, 85 percent of the forest birds (become) _____ extinct or endangered since 1850. Some (die) _____ from avian malaria, which was brought into Hawaii by imported birds. Others (kill) _____ by roof rats, which (introduce) _____ into Oahu in the 1870s.

Kauai

Oahu

Maui

Hawaii

7 **Editing.** There is a mistake in some of the sentences below. Underline the mistake and then write the sentence correctly. Write **Correct** on the line under the sentences with no mistakes.

1. The number of sea urchins began increasing when the otters started to disappear.
   _____*Correct*_____

2. The water hyacinth, that grows in rivers, is difficult to control.
   _____

3. Since explorers brought the water hyacinth from South America, it had spread rapidly.
   _____

4. The sea cow is one animal that it likes to eat the water hyacinth.
   _____

5. Sugar cane is grew in warm climates.
   _____

6. If you allow rats into a field of sugar cane, they would destroy it.
   _____

7. By 1872, the rats have disappeared from the island of Jamaica.
   _____

8. In the early 1800s, there was many buffalo herds in North America.
   _____

9. Buffalo hides were used to make shoes and other leather goods.
   _____

10. Before the white hunters had come to the plains, the buffalo roamed the area in large numbers.
    _____

11. There were so few animals left that they have to pass laws to protect them.

_____

12. It is against the law to fish in that lake and they do anyway.

_____

13. Some of the plants that they brought them here couldn't survive.

_____

14. If they don't stop hunting the otter, it would have been eliminated completely.

_____

15. There are some types of fish that no one has ever seen.

_____

8 **Vocabulary.** Choose the best answer to complete the sentence or answer the question. Circle the letter of your answer.

1. Nick **depends on** his brother. He says,
 a. "I really like my brother."
 b. "My brother is not around very much."
 c. "I couldn't take care of the business without my brother."

2. Alicia can't **get rid of** her headache. She says,
 a. "This headache won't go away."
 b. "I just got a headache."
 c. "I feel better now."

3. Why shouldn't you eat something that is **poisonous**?
 a. It doesn't taste good.
 b. It might kill you.
 c. It will make you tired.

4. Bob went to get his car, but it had **disappeared**. He asked,
 a. "Where did it go?"
 b. "Where did I go?"
 c. "What did I do with my keys?"

5. When I called about a job, they told me to look **elsewhere**. They said,
 a. "We need someone right away."
 b. "We don't have any jobs right now."
 c. "Why don't you come in tomorrow?"

6. What do you think the store did to **attract** customers?
 a. It raised the prices.
 b. It closed the doors.
 c. It gave away free gifts.

7. The child wanted to get his mother's **attention**, so he
   a. started crying.
   b. fell asleep.
   c. sat down.

8. Which of these is an example of a **shelter**?
   a. tepee
   b. toy
   c. tool

9. Which of these is a **source** of heat?
   a. fire
   b. a blanket
   c. gold

10. What might cause a **lack of** water in an area?
    a. too little rain
    b. too much snow
    c. too many rivers

11. The doctor told Danny to change his **diet**. In other words, the doctor wanted Danny to
    a. change what he ate.
    b. change what he wore.
    c. start an exercise program.

12. To avoid **starvation**, what did the travelers take with them?
    a. plenty of warm clothing
    b. some good books
    c. plenty of food

9 **Writing.** Would you make a good salesperson? To find out, brainstorm a list of things that you bought recently or that you would like very much to buy. Next, chose one of these items and freewrite about it for several minutes. Just write whatever comes to mind about the item. Then, write a paragraph in which you try to convince one of your classmates to buy this item. Think about the questions below as you write. Ask a classmate to read your paragraph, and use this person's suggestions when you rewrite your paragraph.

- Who is going to read your paragraph?
- What is your purpose in writing?
- Why is the item that you are writing about worth buying?
- How can you use this item?
- How much will it cost?
- How long will it last?

Name _____ Date _____

_____
_____
_____
_____
_____
_____
_____
_____
_____
_____
_____
_____

10 **Pairwork.** Make sentences showing a connection between the objects in the square below. In the empty square, identify three objects and ask your classmate to connect them.

Example:

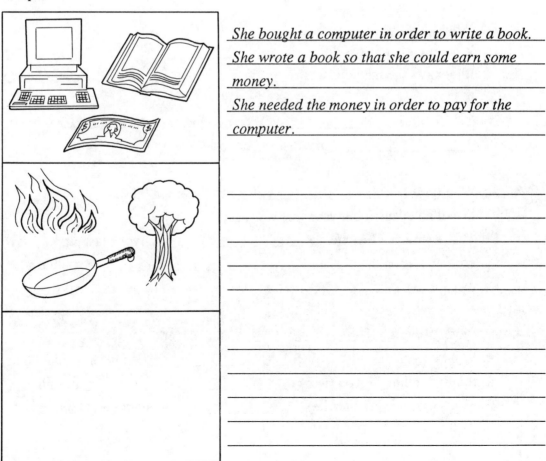

She bought a computer in order to write a book.
She wrote a book so that she could earn some money.
She needed the money in order to pay for the computer.

Cities

1 **Conversations** *(text, exercise 2).* Complete the conversations below, using an appropriate tense of the verb in parentheses. More than one answer may be correct.

1. A: How long (you/live) *have you been living* here?
   B: For two years only. Before I moved here, I (live) _____ in San Diego.

2. A: What (you/do) _____ now?
   B: What do you think I (do) _____?
   A: It looks as though you (wash) _____ the dishes, but I can't believe it.
   B: You (make) _____ fun of me. I know I (not/wash) _____ the dishes very often.

3. A: Who (you/talk) _____ to last night? I (try) _____ to call all evening but your line was busy.
   B: That's strange. I (not/call) _____ anyone last night. Maybe my brother was on the phone. He (use) _____ the phone a lot since he met Julia.

4. A: (you/still/write) _____ that paper?
   B: What do you mean? I (work) _____ on it for just an hour.
   A: Really? I thought you (work) _____ on it this morning.
   B: No. This morning I (write) _____ a letter to Gina.

2 **An interview** *(text, exercise 3).* Read this interview and complete the sentences with an appropriate tense of the verb in parentheses.

Interviewer: Today, we (talk) _____*are talking*_____ with Dr. Phyllis Lee, who is the author of *The Architectural Guide to the Great Antiquities of the World.* Dr. Lee, I (understand) _____ that you have traveled all around the world.

Dr. Lee: Yes, I (guess) _____ I have.

Interviewer: I (imagine) _____ that you have seen all of the great cities of the world.

Dr. Lee: Well, not quite all of them, but I (believe) _____ that I have seen many of the cities of major architectural importance.

Interviewer: I hear that now you (think) _____ of starting a new project. Can you tell us a little about it?

Dr. Lee: I (not/think) _____ I should say anything about it yet.

Interviewer: Now, you (be) _____ very secretive.

Dr. Lee: Not really. I just (feel) _____ that it's too early to say anything. However, I can say that at the moment I (consider) _____ doing something right here in the United States.

Interviewer: That sounds interesting. I (think) _____ many people will be interested in reading about American architecture.

Dr. Lee: I (hope) _____ so.

Interviewer: Well, I (understand) _____ that you are going to show us some slides of your favorite cities around the world. Let's get started.

3 **What are your plans?** *(text, exercise 4).* Imagine that the president of the United States is coming to visit your town or city. The local newspaper has asked you to call the president's assistant to find out more about the visit. Write the questions that you would ask on the lines below. Try to use the future continuous tense. Then have your classmate answer the questions as the president's assistant might.

1. Question: _Where will you be staying?_ _____

   Answer: _____

2. Question: _____

   Answer: _____

3. Question: _____

   Answer: _____

4. Question: _____

   Answer: _____

5. Question: _____

   Answer: _____

4 **Cities in history** *(text, exercise 5).* Make sentences with *who, which,* and *that.* Add commas to set off the non-identifying clauses. In some sentences there is more than one correct answer.

1. The ancient city of Ur, ___*which*___ contained many of the functions of modern cities, was founded in 3500 B.C. It had an enormous temple _____ stood in the center of the city.

2. Many medieval cities were surrounded by walls _____ served as protection from invading forces. In times of danger, the people _____ lived in the area could gather inside the walls for safety.

3. In the 19th century, the Industrial Revolution _____ occurred in Western Europe accelerated urbanization. The city _____ had mainly been a center for trading became a center for industry. The people _____ came to the city in the 19th century had to deal with problems of housing, sanitation, education, and congestion.

4. A major problem confronting cities today is persuading people _____ are doctors, teachers, and government employees to live in the inner city. City planners _____ understand this problem are trying to make the city center a more attractive place in _____ to live. As a consequence, many people _____ moved out of the city in the 1960s and 1970s are now returning.

Name _____   Date _____

5 **Famous structures** *(text, exercise 6).* Complete these sentences with an appropriate tense of the verb in parentheses; use the passive voice.

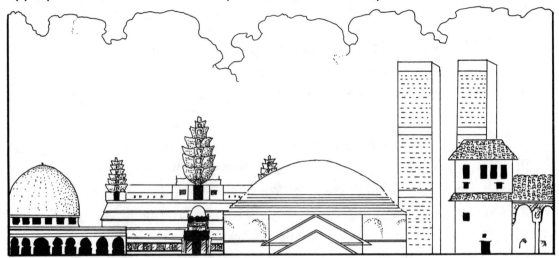

1. The group of pyramids outside of Cairo, Egypt (often/call) ___*is often called*___ one of the wonders of the world. The largest of these pyramids (build) _____ around 2800 B.C.

2. The Parthenon in Athens, Greece (complete) _____ by 438 B.C.

3. If you go to Rome, you should visit the Pantheon. This temple (use) _____ as a place of worship for the past 20 centuries.

4. The Great Wall of China (design) _____ as a means of defense against outside tribes. Today, it (no longer/use) _____ as a means of defense but is instead a popular tourist attraction.

5. The sanctuary called Angkor Wat (think) _____ to be one of the finest examples of Khmer architecture. It (build) _____ in the 12th century.

6. The Alhambra in Granada, Spain, (consider) _____ by many to be the best example of Moorish architecture in the world.

7. The 17th century Taj Mahal (build) _____ by Shah Jahan as a tomb for his wife. This monument (make) _____ entirely of marble.

8. Many people are familiar with the Rouen Cathedral in France because pictures of it (paint) _____ by Claude Monet.

9. The 110-story World Trade Center in New York City (complete) _____ in 1973.

10. St. Mark's Cathedral in Venice is one of the great examples of Byzantine architecture. Part of the cathedral (destroy) _____ by fire in 976, but it (rebuild) _____ later.

11. The Dome of the Rock is located in the city of Jerusalem. This mosque, which (complete) _____ in 691, has a dome which (make) _____ entirely of wood.

6 **Conversations** *(text, exercise 6).* Complete these conversations with an appropriate tense of the verb in parentheses, using either the active or passive voice.

1. A: Don't touch that wall. It (just/paint) *has just been painted* .

   B: Thanks for telling me. I almost (touch) _____ it.

2. A: Excuse me. Do you have any fresh bread?

   B: Just a minute please. It (just/deliver) _____ .

3. A: Where are all the schoolchildren today?

   B: They (take) _____ to a museum in town.

4. A: What happened to that restaurant near your house?

   B: It (close) _____ by the health department.

5. A: This is a beautiful photograph. Where (it/take) _____?

   B: Do you really like it? I (take) _____ it in San Marino.

6. A: Is this your wallet? It (find) _____ on the sidewalk.

   B: Who (find) _____ it?

   A: I don't know. The police (not/tell) _____ me.

7. A: Excuse me, officer. I can't find my car.

   B: Where (it/park) _____?

   A: Right here. I (leave) _____ it here an hour ago.

   B: Then it (move) _____ by the traffic police. This (be) _____ a no-parking area after 4 P.M.

7 **Editing.** There is a mistake in some of the sentences below. Underline the mistake and then write the sentence correctly. Write **Correct** on the line under the sentences with no mistakes.

1. San Francisco which is the gateway to the West enjoys pleasant weather most of the year.

   San Francisco, which is the gateway to the West, enjoys pleasant weather most
   of the year.

2. The mayor has promised that a number of the homeless people will be helping by the agency.

   _____

3. Tomorrow night, the apartment owners will be asked the mayor for an end to rent control.

   _____

4. So much people live in the city that it's impossible to park.

_____

5. I am understanding that the city will be improving the train system.

_____

6. Some people are thinking that the city is not a good place to raise children.

_____

7. If they had known that the cost of housing was going to go up so fast, they wouldn't sell their house.

_____

8. No one dislike living in a city more than my brother.

_____

9. If the rents go down, more people may move back into the city.

_____

10. I am thinking of moving into a building, which is in the center of the city.

_____

11. When the walls built, there were few people living in the city.

_____

12. Many medieval cities, such as Salzburg, still has some of the old walls.

_____

13. During the nineteenth century, rich people began moving to the outer areas of cities.

_____

14. Anyone who live in the city is aware that problems still exist.

_____

15. In the future, it may be possible to have cities that they are built on the ocean.

_____

8 **Vocabulary.** Choose the best answer to each question. Circle the letter of your answer.

1. Joshua **bent over backwards** to help us get the work done. In other words, he
   a. refused to do anything at all.
   b. did everything he could.
   c. did everything wrong.

2. When George explained what had happened, his father **hit the roof.** George asked his father,
   a. "Why did you destroy the roof?"
   b. "Why are you so happy?"
   c. "Why are you so angry?"

3. Their house is located **off the beaten track**.
   a. It's easy to get there.
   b. It doesn't take long to get there.
   c. It takes a while to get there.

4. Susan doesn't want to **stick her neck out** to help her brother. She says,
   a. "I'm not going to help you because I might get into trouble."
   b. "I don't have any money to give you."
   c. "I can't help you because I don't have time."

5. The government is trying to reduce the amount of **red tape** involved in applying for citizenship. The government says,
   a. "We are trying to make the process easier."
   b. "We want to make it harder for people to become citizens."
   c. "We are running out of red tape."

6. When Jeff asked for fifty dollars, his brother said that he couldn't **swing** it. He said,
   a. "I can't refuse you."
   b. "I don't understand you."
   c. "I can't afford it."

7. Diane **ran into a brick wall** when she asked her mother if she could go to Europe. She said,
   a. "My mother won't consider letting me go."
   b. "My mother keeps changing her mind."
   c. "My mother is very eager for me to go."

8. In the United States, the Department of **Commerce** takes care of issues dealing with
   a. culture.
   b. archaeology.
   c. business.

9. A person who is **underfed**
   a. is too fat.
   b. is not getting enough to eat.
   c. should be eating less.

10. In the United States, the Department of **Defense** is responsible for
    a. commerce.
    b. cultural institutions.
    c. the army.

Name _____   Date _____

9 **Writing.** Go to a park, café, or some other public place and watch what is going on. Take notes on all your observations. Later, try freewriting about the scene for a few minutes. Next, write a paragraph in which you present the scene to one of your classmates. Concentrate on tying the sentences in your paragraph together. Then, ask a classmate to read the paragraph and point out anything that is unclear. Use your classmate's suggestions as you write a final draft on the lines below.

_____

_____

_____

_____

_____

_____

_____

_____

_____

_____

_____

_____

10 **Pairwork.** Imagine that you are a tour guide. With your partner, plan a trip to five cities anywhere in the world. Try to convince the rest of the class to take this trip. Explain why you chose these five cities and tell about what they will see on the trip.

Unit 7

1 **Who said it?** *(text, exercise 2).* Read each direct quotation below. Choose the person who most likely made the statement and write a sentence using indirect speech. Use each occupation only once.

> author   archaeologist   dentist   doctor   farmer   pilot   salesperson
> football player   librarian   movie star   musician   student   policeman

1. "I will have to pull it out."
   The dentist said that he would have to pull it out.

2. "You have an overdue book."
   _____

3. "I'm sick of giving autographs."
   _____

4. "I think it's broken, but we will have to take an x-ray to know for sure."
   _____

5. "I missed a few notes, but no one noticed."
   _____

6. "I hope it rains soon."
   _____

7. "I think it's about 2000 years old."
   _____

8. "I'm too tired to play."
   _____

9. "If you look to the right, you will see the Rocky Mountains."
   _____

10. "That dress fits you perfectly."
    _____

11. "I forgot to do my homework."
    _____

12. "I have a great idea for a book."
    _____

13. "You went through a red light."
    _____

Name _____ Date _____

2 **Expressions** *(text, exercise 2).* Choose a quotation from the list below to complete each sentence. Change the direct speech to indirect speech. More than one answer may be appropriate.

- "You can depend on me."
- "You're nuts!"
- "Things are looking up."
- "You must be kidding!"
- "I got rid of it."
- "I don't want to stick my neck out."
- "Your father will hit the roof."
- "There is a lot of red tape."

---

1. When my mother found out that I had decided to quit school, she said that
   *my father would hit the roof.*_____

2. When I told my friend that I was planning to sail around the world alone, he said that
   _____
   _____.

3. When I asked my brother for help, he said that _____
   _____
   _____.

4. When I asked my cousin how his business was doing, he said that _____
   _____
   _____.

5. When I asked my boss why it was difficult to start a business, he said that _____
   _____
   _____.

6. When I asked my sister about her old car, she said that _____
   _____
   _____.

7. I invited my sister to sail around the world with me, but she said _____
   _____
   _____.

8. I tried to get my brother to complain to his boss about the working conditions, but he
   said that _____
   _____.

3 **What did they tell you to do?** *(text, exercise 3).* Answer the questions, using indirect speech.

1. A: Where are you going to put those books?

   B: My mother told me ___*to put*___ them in the attic.

2. A: What are we going to eat for dinner?

   B: Don't you remember? Ma told us _____ the leftovers in the refrigerator.

3. A: How often do you have to practice your guitar?

   B: Well, my instructor told me _____ for an hour a day, but I don't always have enough time.

4. A: Do you want to eat some of this cake?

   B: No, and you'd better not take any. Mother told us _____ any of it.

5. A: Tell me what this word means in Spanish.

   B: I can't. The teacher told us _____ Spanish in class.

6. A: What color are you going to paint this room?

   B: I don't know. Greg told me _____ it red, but I don't think I could live in a red room.

7. A: When do you have to leave?

   B: Tania told me _____ by nine if I wanted to get there on time.

8. A: How often do you have to take that medicine?

   B: The doctor told me _____ it twice a day.

9. A: Why didn't you wash this in hot water?

   B: My sister told me _____ it in cold water so that it wouldn't shrink.

10. A: Why are you doing this exercise?

    B: _____

4   **What did they say?** *(text, exercise 3).* Read the short dialogues below. Then answer the question, using indirect speech.

> *Example:*   John: Are you tired?
> Sarah: No, I'm not.
>
> What did John ask Sarah?
>
> _John asked Sarah if she was tired._ _____

1. Ted: Have you seen my glasses?
   Barbara: No, I haven't.
   What did Barbara say?

   _____

2. Ernesto: Will you give me a ride?
   Juanita: Yes, I will.
   What did Juanita say to Ernesto?

   _____

3. Sandra: Do you need some money?
   Paul: No, I have some.
   What did Sandra ask?

   _____

4. Rachel: Are you ready?
   Simon: I'll be ready in a few minutes.
   What did Rachel want to know?

   _____

5. Piero: Are you OK?
   Cynthia: No, I hurt my arm.
   What did Cynthia say?

   _____

6. Marla: Did you lock the door?
   Nick: No, I didn't.
   What did Marla ask Nick?

   _____

5 **Remarkable journeys** *(text, exercise 4).* Complete the sentences with an appropriate tense of the verbs in parentheses.

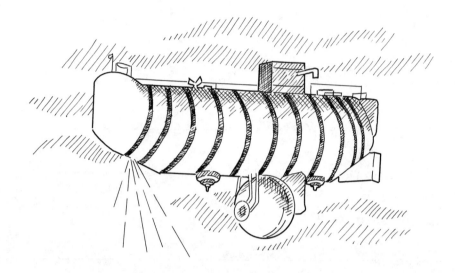

1. According to one book of records, Parke G. Thompson (travel) __*has traveled*__ more than any other American. So far, he (visit) _____ every state in the United States. Outside of the United States, he (travel) _____ to 304 countries and geographical areas out of 308. In 1986, he (be) _____ finally able to go to North Korea, which (not/be) _____ open to western tourists before then. The only areas he (not/visit) _____ are the four Antarctic territories.

2. The first person to reach the North Pole on a solo trip (be) _____ the Japanese explorer Naomi Uemara. He (start) _____ his trip in March 1978 with a sled and 17 dogs. By the time he reached the North Pole, he (travel) _____ 450 miles.

3. In 1911, some Norwegians led by Roald Amundsen (be) _____ the first people to reach the South Pole. After they (reach) _____ the Bay of Whales by boat, they set off for the Pole with dog sleds. It (take) _____ them 53 days to reach the South Pole from the Bay of Whales.

4. Many people (travel) _____ under water. However, the two people who (gone) _____ to the greatest depth are Dr. Jacques Piccard and Lt. Donald Walsh. In 1960, these two men (succeed) _____ in reaching the ocean floor 6.78 miles below the ocean surface. They (make) _____ their trip in a special vehicle called a bathyscaphe. The trip down (take) _____ 4 hours and 48 minutes.

6 **Editing.** There is a mistake in some of the sentences below. Underline the
mistake and then write the sentence correctly. Write **Correct** on the line under the
sentences with no mistakes.

1. The president says that he jogs every day.
    _____ *Correct* _____

2. If I didn't know better, I think that you were angry.
    _____

3. The person whom sent this letter used the wrong address.
    _____

4. My parents don't like us staying out late.
    _____

5. No one except me can describe what happened yesterday.
    _____

6. They were surprised when they saw themself on TV.
    _____

7. The number of tourists to New York and Los Angeles increases every year.
    _____

8. He told me that I could take the car if I want to.
    _____

9. She was considering to go by herself, but then she changed her mind.
    _____

10. If you don't have any goals, you will have trouble making decisions.
    _____

11. He asked me what I would do if I get into trouble.
    _____

12. She learned to depend herself because she had to.
    _____

13. The tapes that are on the table are mine.
    _____

14. She was able to deal with each problem that presented themselves.
    _____

15. Yesterday I did a lot more than I have planned to do.
    _____

16. She asked me if I want to go with her.
    _____

7 **Vocabulary.** Choose the best answer to complete the statement or answer the question. Circle the letter of your answer.

1. I knew my sister was **intrigued** by the idea because she said that
   a. it was a stupid thing to do.
   b. she wanted to find out more about it.
   c. she wasn't interested.

2. Marla tried to **convince** me to go with her. She said,
   a. "You'll have a wonderful time."
   b. "You'll regret it."
   c. "You'll hate it if you go."

3. Why did Alicia say that she couldn't **depend on** her brother?
   a. Because he always does what he says he will do.
   b. Because he doesn't always keep his promises.
   c. Because he has always helped her.

4. Franco hopes to **go far** in his job at a computer company. In other words, he hopes to
   a. move to another company.
   b. do well in his job.
   c. quit his job.

5. Anton found a **rare** coin. He said,
   a. "This is just like all of my other coins."
   b. "This coin is probably not valuable."
   c. "I've never seen one like this."

6. Peter felt **lucky** when
   a. he fell in a hole.
   b. he got the job.
   c. someone stole his wallet.

7. I knew that she had a lot of **spunk** because she told me that
   a. she didn't like to travel.
   b. she preferred to stay at home.
   c. nothing was going to stop her.

8. She told me that she had had a **close call**. Then she described how
   a. her brother had telephoned from downtown.
   b. her car had almost gone off the road.
   c. nothing unusual had happened on the trip.

9. I realized that Felix had a lot of **determination** when he said that
    a. he would never quit trying.
    b. he would never try again.
    c. he was ready to give up.

10. The two soccer players **collided**. In other words, they
    a. raced each other.
    b. ran into each other.
    c. yelled at each other.

8 **Word forms.** Complete these dialogues with the correct form of the words below.

1. collision   collide
    A: Why did the two cars _____*collide*_____?
    B: I don't know, but it was a horrible _____.

2. admiration   admire
    A: I have a lot of _____ for the way he lives his life.
    B: What exactly do you _____ about his lifestyle?

3. success   succeed
    A: Why do you think your business is such a _____?
    B: I think it just takes a lot of hard work to _____.

4. realization   realize
    A: I had a strange _____ last night.
    B: What was that? What did you _____?

5. scare   scary
    A: Do you enjoy _____ movies?
    B: No, I don't enjoy them, but they don't _____ me very much
        either.

6. sincere   sincerely
    A: Were you being _____ when you said that you would help me?
    B: Yes, I said it _____.

9 **Writing.** A paragraph is a group of sentences with a single purpose: to communicate one idea clearly. Usually, a **topic sentence** states the main idea of the paragraph. The other sentences in the paragraph support this idea. In the paragraph below, a student writes about soccer. Read the paragraph and answer the questions that follow.

Skills Needed by a Soccer Player

Soccer players must have many skills in order to be considered good players. For example, they should have the ability to control the ball with their feet, which requires great skill and a strong body. They should also have the ability to execute strong passes to teammates, which demands a strong kicking leg and accuracy. The final and most important skill is the ability to execute a scoring penalty kick, which requires precision and strength.

---

1. Which sentence is the topic sentence in this paragraph? Underline it.
2. The writer gives examples to support the main idea. How many examples did the writer give? _____

Here are some topic sentences. Choose one and freewrite about it for a few minutes. Next, brainstorm a list of examples to support the topic sentence. Then combine the examples with the topic sentence to create a paragraph. Ask a classmate to read your paragraph and to answer the questions in the box.

- There are several things you can do if you have trouble getting to sleep. (Give examples of the things you can do to get to sleep.)
- Learning a new language can be difficult. (Give examples to show how it can be difficult.)
- A dictionary provides more information than just the meanings of words. (Give examples of the types of information that the dictionary provides.)

_____
_____
_____
_____
_____
_____
_____
_____

Name _____   Date _____

_____
_____
_____
_____
_____

Did the writer give several examples?	___ yes ___ no
Are the examples clear?	___ yes ___ no

10 **Pairwork.** Ask one of your classmates the questions below. Then report your classmate's answers on the lines that follow. Use indirect speech. Remember that you can use the present tense when you are reporting information that is always true.

1. What is the most important thing that parents must teach their children?
2. Do you disagree with your parents very often?
3. What is the best age to have children?
4. Were your parents strict?
5. Did your parents ever punish you? If so, what did they do?
6. What did your parents tell you not to do?

Example: Trinh said that the most important thing parents must teach their children is self-respect.

1. _____
   _____

2. _____
   _____

3. _____
   _____

4. _____
   _____

5. _____
   _____

6. _____
   _____

Tests

1 **What did they say?** *(text, exercise 2).* Rewrite the direct quotations below, using indirect speech.

1. "I don't have time to go," Jeff said.
   Jeff said that he didn't have time to go.

2. "You will have a test every Friday," the teacher explained.
   _____

3. "Someone took my wallet," Fernando said.
   _____

4. "I always go to bed early the night before a test," Maurice explained.
   _____

5. "I didn't do any work," Carlos admitted.
   _____

6. "I can't help you because I have to stay late at school," Ted explained.
   _____

7. "I will be late," Susan explained when she called me on the phone.
   _____

8. "We will finish this book soon," the teacher explained.
   _____

9. "It's too cold to go outside," Gabriel said.
   _____

10. "I haven't had time to call," Susan said.
    _____

2 **Questions** *(text, exercise 3).* Write direct questions for the answers below. More than one correct question is possible.

1. Where ___*did you put my suitcase?*_____
   I put it in the car.

2. When _____?
   I have to leave by nine.

3. _____?
   In Hawaii.

4. _____?
   It's my brother's car.

5. _____?
   My sister picked me up.

6. _____?
   I stayed at home and read.

7. _____?
   I didn't go because I was tired.

8. _____?
   I think it belongs to Shirley.

9. _____?
   I think Ernesto took it.

10. _____?
    I'd like to go to the movies.

3 **I don't know!** *(text, exercise 4).* Complete the statements below with an included question.

1. What does she want?
   I don't know ___*what she wants.*_____

2. What did she say?
   I didn't hear _____

3. How old is he?
   I have no idea _____

4. How many children do they have?
   I don't know _____

5. Why did she leave so early?
   I really can't explain _____

6. Why did she quit school?

She didn't tell me _____

7. Why did the teacher cancel classes today?

No one knows for sure _____

8. How many people took the test?

I couldn't find out _____

9. When did they arrive?

They wouldn't tell me _____

10. Whose car is that?

I don't know _____

11. Did he get there on time?

I have no way of knowing _____

12. Where is he taking the French course?

I would like to find out _____

4   **Could you tell me?** *(text, exercise 5).*   Read each of the situations below. Write the question that you would ask. Use included questions.

1. You are standing at the bus stop with several other people. The bus usually comes at 8:00 A.M. You think that it is after 8:00 A.M., but you are not sure. What do you ask?

   Could you tell me what time it is?

   _____

2. You can't remember the details of your homework assignment, so you call a friend for help. What do you ask?

   _____

   _____

3. You plan to go to the movies tonight but you don't know the movie schedule. What do you ask when you call the theater?

   _____

4. You are trying to find State Street but you don't have a map. You see a policeman and ask for information. What do you ask?

   _____

5. Your instructor is going to give the class a test sometime this week. What do you ask to find out exactly when?

   _____

6. You are at a store and you want to buy a shirt. However, none of the shirts has a price tag. What do you ask the clerk?

   _____

7. You are having dinner at a friend's house. The spaghetti you are eating is delicious and you want the recipe. What do you ask your friend?

   _____

8. You don't know the hours of the library, so you call to find out. What do you ask?

   _____

5 **Conversations** *(text, exercise 5).* Complete the conversations below. Use an appropriate tense of the verb in parentheses.

1. A: (you/hear)_*Have you heard*_____ from Dario yet?
   B: No, I _____.
   A: That's strange. I don't understand why (no one/hear) _____ from him for the past two weeks.
   B: I wouldn't worry about it. He told me that he probably (not/call) _____ for a few weeks.

2. A: Do you know why (Jim/not/come over) _____ yesterday?
   B: I think he said that he (have to) _____ work yesterday.

3. A: Do you remember what (Maria/tell) _____ us to bring?
   B: I'm trying to remember. I think she said that we (have to) _____ bring some fruit and cheese.

4. A: Why (we/have to) _____ get up so early?

   B: Don't you remember where (we/have to) _____ go today?

   A: Oh, now I remember. June said that we (have to) _____ be at the airport by noon.

5. A: Where (George/see) _____ Luisella?

   B: He said that he (see) _____ her at the telephone company.

   A: At the telephone company? (she/work) _____ there now?

   B: He didn't tell me what (she/do) _____ there.

6 **Editing.** There is a mistake in some of the sentences below. Underline the mistake and then write the sentence correctly. Write **Correct** on the line under the sentences with no mistakes.

1. Where <u>has</u> you been living since you got married?

   Where have you been living since you got married?

2. Can you tell me where I can buy film?

   _____

3. It helps to know what are your goals.

   _____

4. It's a good idea thinking positive thoughts while you are taking a test.

   _____

5. If he didn't fail the test, he would have passed the course.

   _____

6. Not everyone who take the test passes it.

   _____

7. When he moved here, he hasn't had much money.

   _____

8. She explained that she works as a computer specialist the year before.

   _____

9. One of the teachers claims which she has found a better way to teach math.

   _____

10. I certainly don't understand why did he do so poorly on the test.

    _____

11. She is known for to speak out against unfair working practices.

    _____

12. He has to take several education courses so that he could get his teaching credentials.

    _____

13. She thought that studying all night will help her to pass the test.

_____

14. Many students that they took the exam did very well.

_____

15. I can't tell you why he left as early as he did.

_____

7 **Vocabulary.** Choose the best answer to complete the statement or to answer the question. Circle the letter of your answer.

1. Aurelia thought the movie was **mediocre**. In other words, she thought that it was
   a. a great movie.
   b. terrible.
   c. neither good nor bad.

2. Philip doesn't think his math course is very **challenging**. He says,
   a. "This course is hard."
   b. "This course is easy."
   c. "This course is mediocre."

3. José is **confident** that he will pass the test. He says,
   a. "I'll never pass the test."
   b. "I'm sure I'll pass the test."
   c. "I'm not sure I'll pass the test."

4. Emilo is going to **stick with** the course. He says,
   a. "Nothing will get me to quit."
   b. "I can't finish this course."
   c. "I have to quit."

5. Maria was **astonished** when she heard the news. She said,
   a. "I can't believe it."
   b. "It is just what I expected."
   c. "I knew this would happen."

6. I invited Shirley to go swimming but she said she **wasn't up to it**. She explained that she
   a. didn't enjoy swimming.
   b. had just been swimming.
   c. was too tired.

7. Warren helps to **support** his mother. He says,
   a. "I take my mother wherever she wants to go."
   b. "I give my mother money each month."
   c. "I visit my mother as often as I can."

8. Mahmoud's English has improved **considerably**. The teacher says,
   a. "His English is much better."
   b. "His English is improving slowly."
   c. "His English has improved a little."

9. Marta couldn't **face** looking at her test score. She said,
   a. "I don't want to know what my score was."
   b. "I think my test score is wrong."
   c. "I was unhappy with my test score."

10. During a test, Roger finds it hard to **keep his cool**. He says,
    a. "I don't enjoy taking tests."
    b. "I get nervous during a test."
    c. "I'm usually relaxed during a test."

8 **Writing.** Read the topic sentences below. The general topic in each of these sentences is learning a foreign language. Each writer, however, is going to approach the topic differently.

Writer #1: Learning a new language requires discipline.
Writer #2: There are several good ways to learn a foreign language.
Writer #3: Watching television can help you to learn a new language.
Writer #4: Learning a foreign language can help you professionally.

Imagine that you are going to write a paragraph about each of the general topics below. Write a topic sentence that shows how you will approach each topic. Be specific because you are writing a topic sentence for one paragraph, not for an entire book.

1. the Olympic Games
   The number of sports events in the Olympic Games has changed over the years.

2. friends
   _____

3. learning to drive
   _____

4. marriage
   _____

5. cities

_____

6. tests

_____

Choose one of the topic sentences above and write a paragraph with sentences to support your topic sentence. Ask a classmate to read your paragraph and to answer the questions in the box. Rewrite the paragraph using your classmate's suggestions.

_____
_____
_____
_____
_____
_____
_____
_____
_____
_____
_____
_____
_____

Do all of the sentences in the paragraph support the topic sentence?	___ yes	___ no
Did the writer give several examples?	___ yes	___ no
Is the paragraph convincing?	___ yes	___ no

9 **Pairwork.** People often use included questions when they ask for information. Imagine that one of you is new in the area and you want to get information about one of the items below. With your partner, role-play a dialogue for the rest of the class. Use several included questions and statements in your dialogue.

- Ask for the nearest bank.
- Ask for the name of a good restaurant in the area.
- Ask about the public transportation system.
- Ask for a store that sells sports equipment.

Unit 9

What's Next?

1 **Wishes** *(text, exercise 2).* What do you think these people are wishing? Write your ideas on the blank lines.

1. I wasn't looking and I backed my car into a tree.
   I wish that I ___*had looked behind me.*___

2. His essays are usually so messy that his teacher can't read them.
   His teacher wishes _____

3. I can't go out tonight because I have to study for a test.
   I wish _____

4. Joshua took a job with a small company. Two months later the company went out of business.
   _____

5. When Sandor finished painting the room, he realized that he didn't like the color.
   _____

6. Simon didn't get to play in the soccer game because he arrived late.
   _____

7. My car broke down a week after I bought it.
   _____

8. Nancy wants to get her driver's license, but she isn't old enough.
   _____

9. He ate so much that he got a terrible stomachache.
   _____

10. Laura didn't like her new haircut at all.
    _____

Name _____ Date _____

2 **What are you wishing?** *(text, exercise 2).* Match the phrases on the right with the situations on the left.

_b_ **1.** It's very hot in here. I wish   **a.** they would call.

____ **2.** I didn't have time to finish   **b.** someone would open a window.
      my homework. I wish   **c.** you would give me a ride.

____ **3.** I'm beginning to worry about   **d.** I had been there.
      them. I wish   **e.** you would slow down.

____ **4.** You are walking too fast and I   **f.** I had started it earlier.
      can't keep up. I wish   **g.** you would put him outside.

____ **5.** This table is too heavy for me   **h.** someone would help me.
      to move by myself. I wish

____ **6.** I'm too tired to walk to school
      today. I wish

____ **7.** This dog is driving me crazy.
      I wish

____ **8.** Kevin called but I wasn't at
      home. I wish

3 **Hopes** *(text, exercise 3).* What do you hope will happen? Write your ideas on the blank lines.

1. I haven't received any mail in weeks. I hope _to get some mail soon._

2. My sister has been sick for over a week. I hope _that she gets well._

3. My brother has applied to several universities. I hope _____

4. One of my friends lost her passport. I hope _____

5. I don't have my driver's license yet. I hope _____

6. I can't visit you today, but I hope _____

7. If my father retires from his job, he will have more time to enjoy himself. I hope

_____

8. My brother is thinking about getting married. I hope _____

9. I couldn't take a vacation last year, but I hope _____

10. My sister is going to run in a marathon. I hope _____

11. Two of my friends lost their jobs last week. I hope _____

12. I haven't had time to fix the car. I hope _____

4 **Conversations** *(text, exercise 4).* Complete the conversations below. Use an appropriate tense of the verb in parentheses.

1. A: (you/get) _Will you have gotten___ everything ready by the time the guests arrive?
    B: I think so. I (already/prepare) _____ the food.
    A: And the house (already/clean) _____. I guess we (be)
       _____ ready on time.

2. A: I think we are going to be late. By the time we get there, the concert (start)
       _____.
    B: No, I think your watch (be) _____ fast. We (not/have to)
       _____ leave for another twenty minutes.

3. A: (you/not/finish) _____ that book yet? I want to read it.
    B: Be patient. I (read) _____ as fast as I can. I think I (finish)
       _____ it by dinnertime.

4. A: (you/eat) _____ another candy bar?
    B: Yes. It (be) _____ delicious.
    A: How many (you/eat) _____?
    B: I only (take) _____ four.
    A: Four! At that rate, you (eat) _____ all of them by dinnertime.
    B: No, I (not/eat) _____ any more. I promise.

5 **Conditional statements** *(text, exercise 5).* Complete the dialogues with an appropriate clause.

1. A: Why didn't you get the job?
    B: They said that I didn't have enough experience. If I had had more experience,
       I would have gotten the job.

2. A: Can you come over to my house this evening?

    B: I'd love to but I have a class tonight. If _____,

    I would be glad to come over.

3. A: Did you take my apple?

    B: Was that your apple? Sorry. If I had known it was your apple, _____

    _____.

4. A: Don't you want to go for a walk?

    B: I don't think I'm up to it. If I weren't so tired, _____

    _____.

5. A: Is this your book?

    B: No, I don't think so. If _____,

    it would have my name inside.

6. A: Why didn't you pick me up? Did you forget that I needed a ride?

    B: No one told me that you needed a ride. Believe me, if _____

    _____, I would have picked you up.

6 **Verb tense review** *(text, exercise 6).* Read about the career decisions of the
people below and complete the sentences with an appropriate tense of the verbs in
parentheses.

1. Ernesto (leave) _____*left*_____ school when he was sixteen because he had to
    help support his family. For several years he worked in a restaurant, and by the time he
    was twenty-one he (become) _____ the manager. Lately, he (talk)
    _____ about leaving the restaurant and going back to school, but he
    (not/make) _____ a firm decision yet.

2. Before she went to college, Susan (want) _____ to become a lawyer.
    However, while she (be) _____ in college, she decided to take an art
    course just for fun. The instructor of the course told her that she (have)
    _____ a lot of talent, and he encouraged her (take)
    _____ more art courses. Now she (think) _____
    that she might go to graduate school to study painting.

3. Before my grandmother got her master's degree, she (work) _____ for years teaching young children. In fact, she (teach) _____ for more than forty years when she got her master's degree at the age of sixty-five. Since then, she (work) _____ teaching other teachers.

4. Philip (join) _____ the army when he was twenty years old. By the time he was forty, he (learn) _____ how to fly a helicopter and he (travel) _____ around the world. When he turned forty, Philip (decide) _____ to leave the army so that he could begin another career. Because he was interested in photography, he (go) _____ to film school in Los Angeles. Since he finished the program, he (work) _____ for one of the movie companies in California.

7 **Langston Hughes** *(text, exercise 6).* The sentences below give biographical information about the poet Langston Hughes. Complete the sentences with the appropriate tense of the verbs in parentheses.

1. Langston Hughes (spend) _____*spent*_____ the first years of his life in Kansas with his mother and grandmother. His father (leave) _____ the family and (move) _____ to Mexico before Langston was a year old.

2. By the time Langston was thirteen, his mother (marry) _____ again, and they went to live in Lincoln, Illinois. Within a few months at the new school in Lincoln, Langston (become) _____ the class poet. Soon he (spend) _____ much of his time writing poetry.

3. When he was seventeen, Langston went to Mexico to visit his father. He and his father (be) _____ very different and it was not an easy summer. Langston's father wanted him to become an engineer. Langston, however, had other ideas. He (want) _____ to be a writer since he was thirteen. In the end, Langston (go) _____ to Columbia University to study engineering. He (not/stay) _____ there long, however. Before the year was over, he (decide) _____ to leave the university and to get a job on a boat. Over the next few years, he (travel) _____ to Africa and Europe.

4. When Langston Hughes returned to New York, he (make) _____
   friends with a number of other writers, and he (begin) _____ to sell
   his poems to magazines. Some of his poems (win) _____ prizes, and
   his first book of poetry was soon published.

5. Langston Hughes also (write) _____ plays and essays. Some people
   (describe) _____ his writing as simple and powerful.

8 **Editing.** There is a mistake in some of the sentences below. Underline the mistake and then write the sentence correctly. Write **Correct** on the line under the sentences with no mistakes.

1. I can't understand where <u>did he go</u> after he left here.
   I can't understand where he went after he left here. _____

2. If I could do anything at all today, I would have gone fishing.
   _____

3. George has worked as a lawyer for ten years when he decided to change professions.
   _____

4. By the time they get married, they will have saved enough money to buy a house.
   _____

5. If the students don't want to have a party, we won't have one.
   _____

6. I don't think they are the ones whom should get to go on the trip.
   _____

7. He told me to not go to the park that is near my house.
   _____

8. I didn't understand what he says because he was talking too fast.
   _____

9. If you think you can make me change my mind, you are wrong.
   _____

10. As soon as the game ended, they will come home.
    _____

11. I know several people that they want to join this group.
    _____

12. She thinks he really enjoys to work around the house, but she is wrong.
    _____

13. If you like what you are doing, you would probably do well.
    _____

14. He didn't tell me where he was going and I didn't ask.

_____

15. This table, that is very old, is worth a lot of money.

_____

9 **Vocabulary.** Choose the best answer to each question. Circle the letter of your answer.

1. Luisa **changed her mind** about taking a trip. She said,
 a. "I was going to go, but now I have decided not to."
 b. "I'm still planning to take a trip."
 c. "I have never considered taking that trip."

2. When Piero **retired**, he said,
 a. "Now I will have to start working."
 b. "I'm glad I don't have to work anymore."
 c. "I wish I didn't have to work so hard."

3. It is **unlikely** that she will call tonight. Before she left, she said,
 a. "I will probably call tonight."
 b. "I will not call tonight."
 c. "I probably won't be able to call tonight."

4. Keiko couldn't **figure out** what the salesperson wanted. Keiko said,
 a. "I don't understand what she wants."
 b. "I told her what I wanted."
 c. "She doesn't understand me."

5. Lorenzo found his **niche** when he started teaching. He said,
 a. "This is a difficult job."
 b. "I don't think I'm very good at this."
 c. "This is the perfect job for me."

6. Ahmad thought it was a **waste of time** to learn another language. He said,
 a. "I have no reason to learn another language."
 b. "It takes a long time to learn another language."
 c. "It's useful to know another language."

7. Getting a little nervous before an exam is not **uncommon**. In other words,
 a. it's not normal to get nervous.
 b. a lot of people get nervous.
 c. it's not useful to get nervous.

8. Barbara has some **doubts** about her ability to do the work. She says,
   a. "I know I will like the work."
   b. "I am completely confident that I can do the job."
   c. "I'm not sure I'll be able to do the work."

9. Marta has some **experience** using a computer. She says,
   a. "I have never used a computer."
   b. "I would like to learn to use a computer."
   c. "I have worked on a computer before."

10. Everyone thinks George has a great **imagination** because he
   a. reads well.
   b. has lots of unusual ideas.
   c. can sing very well.

10 **Writing.** Look for upcoming events in the entertainment section of the newspaper or on your school bulletin board. Choose one event that is interesting to you and find out more about it. Then, write a paragraph in which you try to convince your classmates to attend this event. Be sure to include a topic sentence and concentrate on tying the sentences together. In your paragraph, you should also explain the following:

   • where the event will take place
   • when the event will take place
   • who will participate
   • what it will be about
   • why you think it is worth attending

Write the final draft of your paragraph on the lines below. Working with a group of classmates, take turns reading your paragraphs. Together decide which paragraphs are convincing.

_____

_____

_____

_____

_____

_____

_____

_____

_____

_____

11 **Pairwork.** Get your partner to assess his or her English-language abilities by answering the questions below. Then find out what your partner plans to do about studying English in the future. Add questions to the chart below and fill in your partner's answers. Report your findings to the rest of the class.

Your partner's name: _____

Questions	Answers
1. How would you assess your ability to speak English?	_____
2. Which skill are you best at: writing, speaking, reading, or listening?	_____
3. Which skill do you need to practice most?	_____
4. _____	_____
5. _____	_____
6. _____	_____
7. _____	_____
8. _____	_____
9. _____	_____
10. _____	_____